420 DINER
What's On The Menu?

By
LisaMarie Costanzo

BACK STORY

On my thirty-ninth birthday I was given a diagnosis of Multiple Sclerosis. This was not only a wake-up call that life is short, but it caused me to re-evaluate and prioritize everything. I made a realization that those who do not lift us up tear us down, and I needed to purge the weight of negativity. No more heavy sighs.

Needing a temperate climate, I did some research to decide where I wanted to spend the rest of my days. I was strongly drawn to Oregon where I am now blessed with the magical trio: ocean, mountains, and medical marijuana.

Having lost my mother to lung cancer, the idea of ingesting pot rather than smoking it made more sense. Couple that with the fact that ingested marijuana goes into your bloodstream rather than your nervous system, causing a slower but longer-lasting high, and I was ready to taste-test some magical goodies.

However, the "med-ibles" that were readily available were not always very tasty and certainly not something I would serve to company (wink). I needed to roll up my sleeves and get out my own trusty cooking utensils and pans.

I have always loved to cook and ran a catering business back in the day. This gave me a fabulous opportunity to hone my skills. I wanted to make magical goodies that would be desirable to not just me but also to the frou-frou masses, something beyond the typical brownies or Scooby Snacks. Magic Manicotti, anyone? Maybe some Puff Puff Pass Petit Fours? Oh, yeah!

A tiny bit of science: for cooking purposes, THC is both fat-soluble and unable to be released without binding to either fatty acids or alcohol. That said, each of the following recipes will use some form of ingestible marijuana whether it's in butter, oil, or alcohol. Don't worry; I'll walk you through it. Of course, you could always cheat and get it ready-made at the dispensary...

How awesome is it that—as of this writing—two states have legalized recreational marijuana, and the use of medical marijuana is legal in twenty states? It's an exciting time, gang!

Despite everything else, I feel like I have won the karmic lottery. I am able to do things that make me happy every single day. I can hear the ocean from my back porch. I can see the mountains from the patio. If I wake up in the morning and my fingers wiggle, it is going to be a great day.

I am lucky enough to be supported and loved by two amazing children who make me so very proud. Additionally, I have the world's greatest husband. Seriously.

This magical cookbook is for them. I love you, Gabi, Brody, and Tim. Thank you.

Oh, and thank you, Martha.

A LA CARTE

Starters   6-9

Beverages   10-19

Dips/Spreads   20-29

Entrees   30-47

Sauces   48-57

Sides   58-67

Snacks   68-79

Soups   80-95

Sweets   96-113

Index   114-117

STARTERS

Cooking with cannabis is a lot more than just grinding up some leaves and stems and sprinkling it into your brownie mix. There are certain rules that one must follow…or take the risk of not only ruining a recipe but totally wasting your pot.

Basically, we need to understand that THC, the main active ingredient in marijuana, needs to be extracted with heat into some kind of fatty acid, like butter or oil, before it should be added to any food.

Most dispensaries will have cannabis butter and hash oil on hand, so consider going that easy route for these recipes. If you want a certain strain or need a particular medicinal effect, here are a few simple things to keep in mind when making your own:

1. Whether using the biggest buds or leftover leaves and stems, you must grind that stuff up. Use a coffee grinder or a food processor to get the material as close

to a powder consistency as possible. Store your magical flour in a salt shaker and have it at the ready.

2.   Slow low heat is the key. Melt your butter in a double-boiler. Simmer your oil on the lowest setting. Let it do what it needs to do for as long as it needs to do it (2-6 hours). Do not overheat!

3. You will need to strain the mixture once it comes off the heat. Use cheesecloth or a coffee filter to get out any remaining stems, leaves, or powder. These things are now useless as the THC has been leached out and into the butter/oil.

Magic butter is made with 2-3 sticks of butter per ounce of weed. Melt the butter, add the pot powder, and simmer. Period.

Magic oil can be made with any oil other than olive oil (it doesn't heat well). Sprinkle the pot powder in a frying pan, and cover with the necessary amount of oil to cover the weed. Simmer then turn on lowest heat.   Stir occasionally with a wooden spoon.

Magic milk is another great option. An ounce of weed simmered in a crock pot with coconut milk (great high fat content) will make for yummy shakes or even to drink alone. Coconut milk comes in cans, or it is a breeze to make your own.

For recipes that do not use heat (like truffles and cake frosting), tincture is the way to go. In tinctures, the THC is bound to alcohol and is traditionally used by dropper under the tongue. It makes a great sweetener, too, however, and can be added to beverages and soups easily.

Magic tincture is made using a bottle of alcohol with at least an 80 proof/40% alcohol content. Grain alcohol is great for the high alcohol content, but vodka works just as well. Grind your materials to the consistency that you would for a joint. You do not want powder for your tincture.

Decarboxylate. There's a big important word. It means that we need to heat the weed just hot enough and just long enough to maximize the THC without vaporizing it. A good rule: 240 degrees for an hour.

Decarboxylated material goes into a mason jar along with a pint of alcohol, poured in to cover the weed. Tighten the lid and shake the jar a few times. Put in the freezer for a week, taking the jar out to shake vigorously once or twice a day. While in the freezer, the cannabinoids will dissolve into the alcohol which can then be strained and stored in a tincture bottle in a cool dry place.

Hey, you know how to use a computer, so feel free to look up other methods of making these three vital ingredients yourself. Whether you decide to use a crock pot and glycerin to make your own or just take the easy way out and go buy the stuff, THC extraction is a vital part to magical cooking, so have the proper ingredients prepared and ready to add to your recipes.

Disclaimer: These recipes contain marijuana. As the weed strength will vary, the quantities and measurements may need adjusted. Use your best judgment based on the strain you are using.

BEVERAGES

Baked Banana Smoothie

Bloody MaryJane

Budder Beer

Buttered Bhang

High Chai

Loco Coconut Milk

Monster Milkshake

Pot Hot Chocolate

Snoop Diddy

BAKED BANANA SMOOTHIE

4 T magic butter, melted
2 c milk
⅜ c half-and-half
½ c Greek yogurt, vanilla
2 bananas
2 T chocolate syrup

Mix all ingredients in a blender on high until smooth and creamy.

Add ice cubes and blend until smoothie consistency.

Garnish with a drizzle of chocolate syrup.

BLOODY MARYJANE

2 T magic oil
1 can crushed tomatoes
2 oz vodka
2 T dry white wine
1 T white vinegar
1 clove garlic, crushed
1 c croutons
1 T ground cumin
Worchestershire sauce to taste
Tobasco sauce to taste

Rim a glass with a combination of ground black pepper and garlic salt.

Mix all ingredients in a blender.

Garnish with pepperoncini, green olives, and a celery stalk.

BUDDER BEER

1 T magic butter
2 bottles of beer (nothing too hoppy)
¼ c brown sugar
3 egg yolks

Whisk egg yolks and brown sugar together. Set aside.

Slowly add beer to a saucepan already warmed on medium heat. Simmer until foam is nearly gone.

Add ¼ c of warm beer slowly to egg and sugar mixture, stirring constantly.

Slowly pour egg/sugar/beer mixture back into the saucepan with the remaining warm beer, stirring constantly over medium-low heat.

When beer mixture has thickened, add magic butter. Stir until butter dissolves.

Serve in mugs.

BUTTERED BHANG

½ oz cannabis
¼ c unsalted butter
1 c vodka
1 T brown sugar

Melt butter in a saucepan, crumbling weed into the melted butter. Stir over medium heat for one minute.

Add vodka quickly. Then add sugar.

Continue stirring over medium heat, allowing the sugar to dissolve, ~30 seconds.

Remove from heat and strain.

Sweeten to taste with honey. Add cinnamon and cardamom if desired.

HIGH CHAI

¼ c cannabis (stems are great for this)
2 chai tea bags
1 oz vodka
1 c coconut milk
½ c sugar
1 t vanilla
1 t cinnamon

Carefully open tea bags. Add weed/stems and staple to reclose.

Mix vodka and coconut milk in a saucepan; bring to a boil.

Add tea bags.

Simmer on medium-low heat for ~30 minutes being careful not to scald the milk mixture.

Remove from heat. Add sugar, vanilla, and cinnamon.

Pour over ice.

LOCO COCONUT MILK

1 oz cannabis
2 c unsweetened coconut flakes
4 c hot water

Add hot water and coconut to a blender (can be done in two batches if it won't fit at one time).

Blend on high until thick and creamy.

Strain.

If you are doing two batches, add the first strained coconut back into the second batch in the blender.

Simmer strained coconut milk and cannabis in a crock pot, all day and overnight.

Strain.

Yum.

MONSTER MILKSHAKE

2 T magic butter
½ pint cream
½ pint milk (full fat)
3 scoops ice cream

Heat cream in a saucepan over medium heat, careful not to scorch, ~20 minutes.

Add milk to cream halfway through process (~10 minutes in).

Remove from heat and move to refrigerator to chill down.

In a blender, mix milk mixture and ice cream.

Add candy or fruit as desired.

Blend until thoroughly mixed and smooth.

POT HOT CHOCOLATE

Decarboxylated magic flour
1 c whole milk
½ c light cream
1 serving hot cocoa mix

Mix whole milk and light cream in a saucepan.

Add cannabis.

Simmer on low heat for ~30 minutes being careful not to scald the milk mixture.

Strain into a mug.

Add hot cocoa mix.

Add any desired flavoring or liquor while simmering. Almond extract or kahlua is delicious, and the added alcohol will help dissolve the THC.

SNOOP DIDDY

Decarboxylated magic flour
1½ oz vodka
1 ½ oz lemonade

Shake chilled vodka and decarboxylated cannibis in a shaker until cool.

Strain vodka into a glass filled with ice.

Top with lemonade.

Garnish with a lemon slice and a bud.

DIPS/SPREADS

Baked Bacon Dip

Creamy Guac

Easy Cheesy Ball

Hummus Ho

Pizza Dip in 30 Minutes or Less

Poppin' Jalapeno Popper Dip

Smoked Pimento Cheese

Something Fishy

Spreadin' Crab

BAKED BACON DIP

Decarboxylated magic flour
1 # bacon
1 pkg cream cheese
2 c sour cream
2 c shredded cheddar cheese
1 c chopped scallions

Preheat oven to 240.

Sprinkle bacon slices with magic flour and bake until desired crispiness, flipping and re-sprinkling halfway through.

Crumble bacon and combine with all other ingredients. Spread mixture into a baking dish.

Turn oven up to 400. Cover baking dish with aluminum foil and bake for 25-30 minutes or until bubbly.

Serve with crusty bread or big soft pretzels.

CREAMY GUAC

2 T magic oil
1 avocado
1 T lime juice
½ c Greek yogurt
1 t honey
½ t garlic salt
½ t onion powder
¼ t black pepper
1 jalapeno pepper, minced
1-4 T buttermilk (for thinning)

Mash avocado, magic oil, and lime juice together in a bowl with a fork.

Blend in yogurt and honey.

Season and add jalapeno pepper.

Depending on whether you plan to use this as a dip or a dressing, add the buttermilk to desired consistency.

EASY CHEESY BALL

1 c magic butter
2 blocks cream cheese
2 c shredded cheese
1 small red onion, minced
1 pkg corned beef (the cheap 59-cent bag lunch meat works best), chopped fine
1 t garlic salt
½ t black pepper
½ t paprika
1 c chopped nuts

Blend butter and cream cheese together until smooth.

Add shredded cheese, onion, meat, and spices.

Mix together with your hands. Form into a ball.

Coat the cheese ball in chopped nuts. Serve with your favorite crackers.

HUMMUS HO

5 T magic oil, divided
6 cloves garlic, peeled
1 can chickpeas (don't drain)
½ c plain Greek yogurt
1½ T lemon juice
¼ t garlic salt
¼ t black pepper
¼ t cayenne

Preheat oven to 350.

Toss garlic with 2 T magic oil and spread on cookie sheet. Cover with foil and bake for 45 minutes until soft and browning.

Remove from oven and let cool.

In a food processor, pulse together chickpeas, garlic cloves, lemon juice, and seasonings. Add a little oil to the processor if hummus consistency is too thick.

Pour hummus into a bowl and make a little puddle of remaining oil in the center. Serve with pita chips.

PIZZA DIP IN 30 MINUTES OR LESS

1 c magic butter
½ c sour cream
1 pkg cream cheese, softened
½ c pizza sauce
¼ c chopped onion
¼ c chopped green pepper
½ t garlic salt
¼ t crushed red pepper
½ c chopped pepperoni
½ c shredded mozzarella cheese

Preheat oven to 350.

Mix butter, sour cream, and cream cheese until smooth. Spread in the bottom of a baking dish.

Pour and spread pizza sauce over butter/cheese layer. Add seasonings. Top with pepperoni. Cover with foil and bake for 10 minutes.

Remove from oven. Remove foil. Sprinkle with mozzarella and return to oven. Bake 5 more minutes.

POPPIN' JALAPENO POPPER DIP

Decarboylated magic flour
¼ c magic butter
1 # bacon
2 pkgs cream cheese, softened
1 c shredded cheddar cheese
½ c shredded mozzarella cheese
1 c mayonnaise
1 c diced scallions
4-6 jalapenos, chopped and de-seeded
1 c crushed crackers
½ c shredded parmesan cheese

Coat bacon with flour and bake until desired crispiness. Flip and re-coat midway through the process.

Mix together cream cheese, cheddar and mozzarella cheeses, and mayonnaise. Add scallions and onions. Fold in crumbled cooked bacon.

Spread in a baking dish and cover with aluminum foil. Turn oven up to 400. Bake for 25-30 minutes or until bubbly.

SMOKED PIMENTO CHEESE

¼ c magic oil
1 large red pepper, diced fine
1 c mayonnaise
2 c shredded sharp cheddar cheese
Salt and pepper to taste
¼ t cayenne powder

Preheat oven to 350.

Spread red pepper pieces out on a cookie sheet and drizzle with magic oil. Salt and pepper and bake for 45 minutes.

Remove from oven and cool.

Mix peppers with remaining ingredients and serve at room temperature.

Great on a sandwich.

SOMETHING FISHY

2 T magic oil
2 T mayonnaise
1 lg can tuna in water
3 anchovy fillets, chopped
½ clove garlic, minced
1 lg tomato, cut in half

Mix all ingredients except tomato.

Scoop tuna mixture onto tomato halves.

Broil just until top starts to brown.

SPREADIN' CRAB

1 T magic oil
2 T mayonnaise
1 t Dijon mustard
1 pkg cream cheese
2 c shredded cheddar cheese
¼ t crushed black pepper
¼ t crushed garlic
2 c crab meat, flaked

Preheat oven to 375.

Mix all ingredients together.

Spoon into a baking dish. Sprinkle top with paprika.

Cover with aluminum foil and heat for 15 minutes.

Serve with club crackers or vegetables.

ENTREES

Biscuit Pot Pie

Chicken Enchiladas with Green Sauce

Cranked-Up Carbonara

Doobie Dogs

Jerk Pork

Magic Manicotti

Porky Pig Medallions

Sticky Wings

Super Fried Rice

BISCUIT POT PIE

½ c magic oil
4 T magic butter
1 sm bag frozen mixed vegetables
¼ c frozen peas
4 chicken breasts
½ c flour
1½ c milk
2½ c chicken broth
3 T dry sherry (optional)
½ t garlic salt
½ t black pepper
½ t dried thyme
¼ t parsley

Preheat oven to 400.

Saute chicken breasts in magic oil until no longer pink inside. Remove from heat and put in a bowl. Shred cooled chicken.

Add vegetables (not peas) to sauté pan. Heat, season, and then stir vegetables into bowl of shredded chicken.

Into the same saucepan, melt magic butter. Stir in flour and cook for about a minute. Whisk in milk and chicken broth. Allow to simmer until it starts thickening, about a minute. Add spices as it cooks.

Stir in optional sherry now.

Turn off heat and add chicken mixture, mixing well to combine. Mix in the peas.

Pour the filling into a baking dish. Bake for 18 minutes. Remove baking dish from the oven and top filling with biscuit dough.

Return to the oven for 10-12 minutes, until biscuits are golden brown and the filling is bubbly.

Cool for five minutes before serving.

CHICKEN ENCHILADAS WITH GREEN SAUCE

½ c magic oil
4 chicken breasts, cut into pieces
3 cloves garlic, chopped
2 jars medium green salsa
¾ c heavy cream
12 corn tortillas
3 c shredded Monterey Jack cheese

Preheat oven to 450.

In large saucepan, sauté chicken with magic oil and garlic. Remove from heat.

In a bowl, stir together salsa and cream.

Add ½ c salsa mixture to cooled chicken pan. Combine ingredients.

Prepare tortillas by piling them between damp paper towels and microwaving for one minute.

Working with one tortilla at a time, dip the tortilla in the salsa mixture and then fill it with ½ c chicken mixture. Roll the tortilla and lay in a baking pan, seam side down.

Top tortillas with remaining salsa mixture. Sprinkle with cheese.

Cover with foil and bake for half hour. Remove foil and bake 10-15 more minutes, until brown and bubbling.

Serve with a dollop of sour cream and a garnish of cilantro.

CRANKED-UP CARBONARA

Decarboxylated magic flour
1 T magic butter
1 # bacon
2 chicken breasts, boneless, skinless, cut up
1 c whipping cream
4 eggs
½ c shredded parmesan cheese
1 can peas
1 pkg fettuccini noodles

Coat bacon with flour and bake on 240 until nearly done. Flip and re-coat midway through the process.

Remove bacon from oven and move to saucepan, adding cubes of chicken. Heat thoroughly on medium-high heat until chicken is no longer pink inside and bacon pieces are crispy.

Whisk together cream, eggs, cheese, and melted butter. Stir in peas.

Prepare noodles as directed on the package. Drain and return to pot.

Add sauce mixture and cook on low until sauce starts to thicken, about 2-3 minutes.

Remove from heat and stir in bacon, chicken, and pan juices.

DOOBIE DOGS

Decarboxylated magic flour
¼ c magic butter
1 # bacon
½ c shredded cheese
8 hot dogs
8 hot dog buns

Cut a slit in hot dogs lengthwise. Fill with shredded cheese.

Wrap magic flour-dredged bacon slices around the cheese-filled hot dog. Secure with toothpicks.

Place on a grill until bacon is thoroughly cooked and cheese is melty.

Before serving, lightly "butter" the hot dog bugs and toast them on the grill, too.

JERK PORK

2 T magic oil
½ c soy sauce
¼ c vinegar
½ c orange juice
2 cloves garlic
5 scallions
2 scotch bonnet peppers (wear gloves!)
1 T thyme
2 t salt
½ t black pepper
1 T brown sugar
2 t ground allspice
1 t nutmeg
1 t cinnamon
1 t grated ginger
1 boneless pork loin

Preheat grill to 300.

In a food processor, pulse liquids, vegetables, and spices together to make the marinade.

Cut 1" slits in the pork loin with a paring knife to help with the marinating process.

Wearing gloves, pour 2 cups of marinade over the pork loin in a deep bowl, rubbing it all over and into the slits. Cover and refrigerate ~5 hours.

Brush grill grate with oil and lay pork loin on grate over indirect heat. Fire should be to the side to reduce risk of contact and burning.

Baste every 20 minutes with remaining marinade in the bowl. Grill for 2½ - 3 hours, keeping the lid closed between basting.

Allow to rest before slicing.

MAGIC MANICOTTI

½ c magic oil
1 bunch fresh spinach
1 c shredded mozzarella cheese
15 oz ricotta cheese
4 oz cream cheese
½ c shredded Romano cheese
2 lg eggs
½ t garlic salt
½ t ground black pepper
½ t oregano
1 box manicotti noodles
3-4 c marinara sauce
½ c shredded parmesan cheese (for topping)

Preheat oven to 375.

Sauté spinach with oil over medium heat. Remove from stove.

In a large bowl, mix together cheeses, eggs, and spices. Add sautéed spinach.

Scoop cheese mixture into a pastry bag (or a gallon-size plastic zip bag) and squeeze it into one corner. Snip that corner for piping.

Pour half of the marinara sauce into the bottom of a baking pan and spread to cover the bottom.

Pipe cheese into uncooked manicotti shells, letting it squirt out each end a little. Place filled shells into the sauce-lined pan. Repeat until all shells and filling have been used.

Cover pasta with remaining marinara sauce. Sprinkle top with parmesan cheese.

Cover with foil and bake for an hour. Remove foil to bake last ten minutes.

PORKY PIG MEDALLIONS

Decarboxylated magic flour
1 T magic oil
1 # bacon
2 pork tenderloins
8 oz beer
Ground black pepper, to taste

Sprinkle flour onto a cookie sheet (this step can be done right after decarboxylation).

Dredge bacon in the flour.

Wrap coated bacon slices around pork medallions. Secure the bacon slices with a toothpick or a piece of twine wrapped around the tenderloin.

Cook in magic oil on medium-low heat, turning as necessary to get all sides browned and make sure the pork is thoroughly cooked. Season with black pepper before and after flipping.

De-glaze pan with beer to make a nice sauce to pour over the pork medallions.

STICKY WINGS

2 T magic butter
2 T magic oil
3 # chicken wings
¼ c maple syrup
½ c blackberry preserves
2 T balsamic vinegar
3 T cayenne hot sauce

Preheat oven to 450.

Fill a saucepan with water in preparation for par-boiling chicken wings. Drop chicken into boiling water and boil for 8 minutes.

Remove from water and pat dry.

Lay chicken wings out on foil-lined baking sheet and drizzle with oil. Season with salt and pepper to taste.

Bake for 20-25 minutes (depending on size of wings). Flip in the last five minutes.

Melt butter, syrup, preserves, vinegar, and hot sauce together in a saucepan. Turn heat to low, simmer, stirring continuously.

Remove wings from oven and pour into a large bowl. Cover with sauce, coat well.

SUPER FRIED RICE

1 T magic butter
1 T magic oil
2 eggs
2 c cooked rice (white or brown)
1 carrot, shredded
¼ c red and green bell peppers, chopped
1 stalk celery, chopped fine
3 cloves garlic, minced
1 onion, chopped
½ c frozen peas
¼ t garlic powder
¼ t black pepper
¼ t cayenne
1 T soy sauce
1 chicken breast, cut in cubes
2 boneless pork chops, cut in cubes

Scramble eggs and cook in pan with butter, omelet style. Remove from skillet, cut omelet into strips.

Toss cubes of chicken and pork into a large skillet (wok if you have one) with oil and spices. Stir about two minutes on medium-high heat.

Add carrot, peppers, celery, garlic, and onion. Then add peas.

Add cooked rice and soy sauce.

Mix well.

Finally, fold in strips of egg.

Serve with chopsticks.

SAUCES

Caramel Assault

Gimme Chimichurri

Kickin' Hot Sauce

Lemon Caper Butter

Peach Barbeque Sauce

Peanut Sauce

Righteous Red Sauce

Stir Fried Sauce

Unbelievable Pesto

CARAMEL ASSAULT

¾ c magic butter
2 c sugar
1 c heavy whipping cream
1 T coarse salt

Add sugar to a saucepan on medium heat until sugar starts to melt. Whisk lumps until completely melted and liquid.

When the sugar liquid turns an amber color, add the butter. Whisk until butter is incorporated.

Remove from heat. Slowly stir in cream.

Stir in salt.

Let sit for ten minutes.

GIMME CHIMICHURRI

½ c magic oil
2 c fresh parsley or cilantro
¼ c fresh oregano
5 cloves garlic
2 T chopped onion
2 T red wine vinegar
1 T lime juice
¼ t kosher salt
½ t red pepper flakes

Finely chop herbs, oregano, garlic, and onion. Scoop into a bowl.

Pour in red wine vinegar and lime juice.

Whisk in oil and spices.

Can be put through a food processor.

KICKIN' HOT SAUCE

¼ c magic butter
¼ c hot sauce (chipotle or a flavored tobasco are super yummy)
1 T corn starch

Melt butter in a saucepan on medium-low heat.

Add hot sauce, mix thoroughly.

This sauce can be added to just about anything.

To thicken the sauce and make is a great coating for wings or ribs, add the corn starch. This will thicken the hot sauce mixture and make it stick better to your proteins.

LEMON CAPER BUTTER

2 T magic butter
1 T minced shallot
1 T flour
1 c chicken broth
¼ c dry white wine
1 t grated lemon zest
3 T lemon juice
3 T capers
¼ t ground pepper, black or white
2 T chopped fresh herbs (parsley, cilantro, mint, etc.)

Melt butter over medium heat. Add shallot and cook until tender, stirring, ~2 minutes.

Stir in flour.

Pour in broth and continue stirring.

Add wine, lemon zest, lemon juice, capers, and pepper. Cook until sauce thickens, 3-5 minutes.

Remove from heat. Stir in herbs.

PEACH BARBEQUE SAUCE

1 T magic oil
¼ c chopped shallot
1 c sliced peaches
1 sm jar tomato paste
¼ c apple cider vinegar
¼ c water
2 t soy sauce
¼ t chipotle pepper flakes
½ t salt
¼ t black pepper

Cook shallots in oil until soft, ~5 minutes.

Add remaining ingredients and simmer for 5 minutes.

Transfer to a blender. Pulse until smooth.

PEANUT SAUCE

1 t magic oil
1 T honey
2 T soy sauce
3 T creamy peanut butter
2-3 T half-and-half
1 T chopped scallions

Combine oil, honey, soy sauce, and peanut butter in a bowl.

Add half-and-half, stirring to desired consistency.

Garnish with scallions.

RIGHTEOUS RED SAUCE

2 T magic oil
2 lg cans crushed tomatoes
2 lg cans tomato puree
1 sm can tomato paste
2 T sugar
8 cloves garlic, chopped
1 small onion, chopped
¼ c fresh oregano, chopped
¼ c fresh basil, chopped
¼ c fresh parsley, chopped
½ t garlic salt
¼ t black pepper

Saute garlic, onion, and oregano in magic butter just until fragrance is released

Add remaining ingredients.

Simmer for an hour.

STIR FRIED SAUCE

1 T magic oil
1 t grated fresh ginger
1 t minced garlic
½ c soy sauce
½ c chicken broth
¼ c brown sugar
1½ T rice wine vinegar
1 T toasted sesame oil
1 t sriracha hot sauce
1 T cornstarch
3 T water

Whisk together soy sauce, broth, brown sugar, sesame oil, and sriracha.

In a small cup, dissolve cornstarch in water.

Heat magic oil in a pan, adding ginger and garlic. Cook 30 seconds, stirring constantly, until fragrant. Add soy sauce mixture and bring to a boil. Reduce heat and simmer 3 minutes.

Stir in cornstarch mixture. Boil gently, ~1 minute, until thickened.

UNBELIEVABLE PESTO

¼ c magic oil
3 c fresh basil, packed
3 cloves garlic
¼ c pine nuts
¼ c parmesan cheese, grated

Toast garlic and pine nuts together in a saucepan over medium heat. Shake the pan occasionally to toast nuts evenly.

Place oil, basil, garlic, and pine nuts in a blender and pulse until desired consistency.

Scoop everything into a bowl and stir in cheese.

Salt to taste.

SIDES

Beyond Baked Beans

Broccoli Bud Casserole

Fried Potatoes

Oh Corn

Peas and 'Shrooms

Quinoa Wow

Roasted Green Beans

Sweet Sweet Potato Sticks

Totally Grilled Squash

BEYOND BAKED BEANS

2 T magic butter
1 small onion, chopped
1 small bell pepper, chopped
1 lg can baked beans
1 c brown sugar
1 t garlic salt
1 t black pepper
1 t red pepper flakes

Pour can of beans into a baking dish.

Saute onion and bell pepper with magic butter. Add to beans.

Stir in brown sugar, salt, and peppers.

Cover with foil and bake, 25 minutes.

BROCCOLI BUD CASSEROLE

4 T magic butter, divided
1 T flour
¾ c milk
½ c shredded cheddar cheese
1 pkg frozen broccoli, thawed and drained
½ c bread crumbs

Melt 2 T butter in a saucepan. Add flour and stir, ~1 minute.

Add milk to saucepan, whisk. Bring to a boil being careful not to burn the milk.

Slowly add cheddar cheese, allowing it to melt into the milk mixture.

Add broccoli and heat thoroughly. Pour into a baking dish.

In a small bowl, mix 2 T melted butter with bread crumbs until well combined. Sprinkle bread crumb mixture over broccoli. Sprinkle additional cheese on top.

Broil until cheese melts, ~2 minutes.

FRIED POTATOES

¼ c magic butter
4 potatoes, sliced thin
1 small onion, chopped
1 clove garlic, crushed
1 egg

Saute potatoes, onions, and garlic together with magic butter in a saucepan on medium heat.

Put the lid on to allow the steam to hold vapor and allow the potatoes to cook thoroughly until browned and softened.

Once onions are carmellized, crack an egg on top. Replace lid to allow egg to cook, just 2-3 minutes.

Great to flavor with Kickin' Hot Sauce.

OH CORN

Decarboxylated magic flour
1 c coconut milk
4 ears corn, kernels cut from cob
¼ t salt
2 T fresh cilantro, chopped
1 T lime juice
¼ t crushed red pepper

Simmer coconut milk and flour together for ~30 minutes. Be careful not to scald.

Strain.

Combine corn, milk, and salt in a saucepan. Bring to a boil.

Reduce the heat to an active simmer.

Cook until coconut milk has mostly evaporated, 12-15 minutes.

Stir in cilantro, lime juice, and pepper.

PEAS AND 'SHROOMS

2 T magic butter
1 small onion, chopped
2 cloves garlic, minced
1 pkg frozen green peas, thawed
1 sm jar sliced mushrooms, drained
1 t sugar
½ t salt
¼ t thyme
¼ t black pepper

Cook peas according to package directions. Set aside.

Melt butter over medium heat. Saute onion and garlic until tender.

Stir in peas and mushrooms.

Season with sugar, salt, thyme, and pepper. Reduce heat to low.

QUINOA WOW

2 t magic oil
1 c quinoa
1 small onion, chopped
1 can chopped green chiles
2 cloves garlic, minced
1 c chicken broth
¼ c pepitas, toasted
¾ c fresh cilantro, coarsely chopped
½ c chopped scallions
2 T lime juice
¼ t salt

Prepare quinoa by toasting it in a dry skillet over medium heat, stirring often, until aromatic. Transfer to a fine sieve and rinse.

Saute onion in magic oil. Add chiles and garlic, stirring, ~30 seconds.

Add quinoa and broth, bring to a simmer. Reduce heat, cover, and cook until quinoa is tender, 20-25 minutes.

Add pepitas, cilantro, scallions, lime juice, and salt. Mix gently. Fluff with a fork.

ROASTED GREEN BEANS

¼ c magic butter
1 # fresh green beans
1 small onion
2 cloves garlic, chopped
1 T oregano
½ t cayenne
½ c hazelnuts

Preheat oven to 425.

Trim beans and boil until crisp, ~5 minutes. Drain.

On a baking sheet, drizzle oil over green beans. Add onion and garlic, stir to distribute oil. Season.

Bake to desired doneness, stirring every 10 minutes.

Add hazelnuts just before serving.

SWEET SWEET POTATO STICKS

½ c magic oil
2 lg sweet potatoes, cut into sticks
½ T salt
1 t pepper
¼ t paprika
½ t chili powder
¼ t cinnamon
2 cloves garlic, minced
1 c plain Greek yogurt
2 t lime juice
½ T curry powder

Preheat oven to 425.

Toss sweet potato sticks in a bowl with salt, pepper, paprika, chili powder, cinnamon, garlic, and oil.

Spread on a baking sheet and bake until potatoes are tender, 20-30 minutes. Stir periodically.

While sticks are baking, make dipping sauce in a bowl by combining, yogurt, lime juice, and curry powder.

TOTALLY GRILLED SQUASH

¾ c magic butter
2 zucchini, halved, cut into ½" slices
1 summer squash, thinly sliced
1 T salt
2 T ground black pepper
2 T garlic powder

Preheat grill to medium-high heat.

Place zucchini and squash slices on a large sheet of aluminum foil. Dot with butter.

Season, seal vegetables in foil.

Place folded foil pack on grill for 20-25 minutes, until vegetables are tender.

SNACKS

Caramel Corn Crack

Fluffer Snicker Firecrackers

Garlic Cheese Bread

Nutty Oat Bars

Pepperoni Rolls

Spicy Peanuts

Wonton Crackers

You Say Potato 1

You Say Potato 2

CARAMEL CORN CRACK

Decarboxylated magic flour
3 T magic butter
3 T magic oil
6 slices bacon
½ c popcorn kernels
1½ t baking soda
¾ t cayenne pepper
3 c sugar
2 t sea salt

Preheat oven to 300.

Cover a large bowl and two rubber spatulas in cooking spray. Set aside.

Lay bacon slices on a baking sheet side by side. Coat with magic flour. Bake until just crispy. Cool on a paper towel. Cut into bite-size pieces.

In a large pot with a lid, heat oil over medium-high heat. Add kernels and keep pan moving until all kernels are popped, ~4 minutes. Transfer popped corn to prepared bowl, removing any unpopped kernels.

In a small bowl, whisk together baking soda and cayenne pepper. Set aside.

In a medium saucepan, combine sugar, butter, salt, and ½ c water. Cook over high heat until mixture turns a golden yellow color, ~10 minutes.

Remove from heat. Whisk in baking soda mixture (it will bubble). Quickly fold in bacon pieces.

Pour caramel and bacon over popcorn in bowl, tossing like a salad until popcorn is evenly covered by the caramel.

Pour popcorn out onto a baking sheet to cool. Separate large pieces.

FLUFFER SNICKER FIRECRACKERS

2 t magic oil
2 T peanut butter
2 T marshmallow fluff
¼ c chocolate chips
6 cinnamon graham crackers

Preheat oven to 310.

Mix together oil and peanut butter.

Spread mixture evenly on graham crackers until gone.

Lay crackers on a baking sheet (spread side up). Put a small dollop of marshmallow on each cracker.

Cover with foil. Bake for 23 minutes.

Remove from oven, uncover, and sprinkle with chocolate chips. Allow to sit for 3 minutes. Spread melted chocolate and marshmallow evenly over the crackers.

Sandwich crackers together. Let cool. Eat.

GARLIC CHEESE BREAD

2 c magic butter
1 clove garlic, crushed
1 t oregano
1 t black pepper
½ t cayenne
2 c shredded mozzarella
1 loaf Italian bread, cut lengthwise

Preheat oven to 375.

Mix butter with garlic and spices. Mash together until well blended.

Lay open loaf of bread on aluminum foil lined cookie sheet and slather with butter mixture.

Bake for ten minutes until butter is melted and bread starts crisping on the edge.

Remove from oven and sprinkle cheese over melted butter.

Broil for five minutes or until cheese starts melting.

NUTTY OAT BARS

1 T magic butter
2 T chocolate chips
3 T peanut butter
2 T milk
1 t vanilla
1 T brown sugar
½ c oats
1 T optional: nuts, coconut, seeds, raisins

Melt first three ingredients together in a microwave, stopping to stir every 30 seconds.

Add milk, vanilla, and brown sugar. Combine well.

Mix in oats and optional ingredients. Mixture should be fairly dry. Slowly add more oats if necessary.

Press mixture into a baking sheet lined with plastic. Refrigerate for 20-30 minutes to allow bars to set up. Pull plastic out of pan to lift oat mixture, cut into bars.

PEPPERONI ROLLS

2 T magic butter
¼ t oregano
¼ t garlic salt
¼ t black pepper
1 T grated parmesan cheese
1 pkg refrigerated crescent roll dough
4 cheese sticks, halved
1 pkg pepperoni slices

Preheat oven to 350.

At the bottom of dough triangle, lay 6 slices of pepperoni. Place half a stick of cheese stick on top.

Roll up. Lay on a cookie sheet, seam side down. Bake for 10-14 minutes, until golden brown.

Mix melted butter with seasonings and parmesan cheese.

Brush baked crescent rolls with butter mixture while they cool.

SPICY PEANUTS

1 T magic oil
2 t chili powder
2 t ground cumin
2 t sugar
1 t curry powder
1 t garlic powder
¼ t cayenne
2½ c dry roasted peanuts

Mix spices with oil in a saucepan over medium heat. Stir until fragrant, ~30 seconds.

Add peanuts, stir to coat.

Spread peanuts on a large baking sheet, bake until golden brown and nearly dry, ~15 minutes.

Season lightly with salt.

Transfer to a paper towel to cool.

WONTON CRACKERS

¼ c magic oil
25 wonton wrappers
1 c grated cheddar cheese
2 T dried basil

Preheat oven to 375.

On a large baking sheet, lay wonton wrapper side by side.

Brush with oil. Sprinkle with cheese and basil.

Season with salt and pepper to taste.

Bake for 8 minutes or until crackers start to brown.

For a sweet variation: use butter, cinnamon, and sugar instead of oil, cheese, and basil.

YOU SAY POTATO 1

¼ c magic butter
6 medium potatoes
1 c shredded cheese
Toppings: sour cream, salsa, shredded cheese, chopped scallions, black olives.

Preheat oven to 425.

Scrub potatoes and prick with a fork. Bake 40-60 minutes until tender.

Cut potatoes lengthwise into quarters. Scoop out potato pulp and set aside for YSP2 recipe.

Brush potato skins with melted butter. Broil, skin side up, 3-4" from heat for three minutes.

Turn potato skin side down, brush with butter, and sprinkle with shredded cheese. Broil another two minutes.

Serve with bowls of individual toppings.

YOU SAY POTATO 2

½ c magic butter
Reserved potato pulp from YSP1 recipe
1½ c sour cream
1 envelope ranch dressing mix
1 t garlic salt
1 T dry parsley
3 c grated cheddar cheese, halved
1 c milk

Preheat oven to 350.

Mash potato pulp, leaving a few lumps.

Add butter, sour cream, dressing mix, garlic salt, parsley, 1½ c shredded cheese, and milk. Mix well.

Pour potato mixture into a baking pan, cover with foil. Bake for 20 minutes.

Remove foil and add remaining cheese. Optional now: add bacon bits, scallions, chives. Bake ten more minutes.

SOUPS

Broc-Pot-Leek Soup

Cabbage Comfort

Cheesy French Onion

Corn Cob Chowder

Jewish Penicillin Plus

Lasagna Soup

Rice and Turkey

Veggie Bowl

Wild 'Shroom Soup

BROC-POT-LEEK SOUP

1 T magic oil
8 c water
8 t vegetable base
4 c broccoli florets
½ c onion, diced
6 cloves garlic, finely chopped
2 c leeks, chopped, white part only
1 ½ # potatoes, peeled, diced large
2 # broccoli, chopped
1 t salt
¼ t black pepper

Put water and base on to simmer. Add broccoli florets, blanch until tender. Remove florets from stock, set aside.

In a big cook pot, saute onions in oil on medium heat until translucent. Add garlic, stirring frequently, ~2 minutes.

Add diced leeks. Saute for four minutes.

Add vegetable stock and simmer. Add potatoes, bring to a boil, then lower heat to simmer four minutes.

Add 2 # broccoli and simmer on medium heat until potatoes are fully cooked.

Remove from heat. Blend with a vertical stick blender until pureed.

Garnish with blanched florets.

CABBAGE COMFORT

3 T magic oil
14 oz summer sausage, cut into ½" slices
3 c cabbage, chopped
½ # potatoes, peeled, diced large
5 c chicken broth
1 lg can diced tomatoes
½ t crushed red pepper flakes

Heat oil over medium heat, brown sausage on both sides, 5-7 minutes. Add potatoes and cabbage, stirring occasionally, until cabbage starts to wilt.

Pour in chicken broth and tomatoes with juice. Stir in crushed red pepper, salt and pepper to taste.

If necessary, add water so that liquid covers sausage and potato mixture. Bring to a boil.

Reduce heat and simmer, stirring occasionally until potatoes are tender and flavors have melded, 10-15 minutes.

CHEESY FRENCH ONION

4 T magic butter
5 medium onions, peeled, sliced thin
½ t salt
2 c chicken broth
2 c beef broth
¼ cup dry wine, red or white
2 T chopped fresh parsley
1 T chopped fresh thyme
1 bay leaf
1 T balsamic vinegar
1 loaf French baguette, cut on diagonal, ¾" slices
4½ oz Swiss or gruyere cheese, sliced thin
3 oz grated asiago cheese

Preheat oven to 400.

Sauté onions and salt, stirring occasionally, until thoroughly coated with butter. Reduce and brown, 30-35 minutes.

Stir in both broths, wine, parsley, thyme, and bay leaf. Simmer, stirring bottom of pan with wooden spoon to loosen browned onion bits, ~30 minutes.

Remove and discard herbs. Stir in balsamic vinegar. Salt and pepper to taste.

Arrange baguette slices on a cookie sheet and bake until crisp, ~10 minutes.

Set heatproof bowls on cookie sheet. Fill each with 1½ c soup. Top with two baguette slices and a single layer of cheese over the bread.

Sprinkle with asiago cheese. Place bowls in the oven 5-6" from the broiler. Broil until cheese is brown and bubbly, ~10 minutes.

CORN COB CHOWDER

2 t magic oil
1 small onion, chopped
1¾ c chicken stock
2 ears of corn with kernels cut off plus cobs
¼ t cumin
¼ t coriander
½ t salt
1 t fresh chives, finely chopped
¾ c half-and-half

Heat oil over medium-high heat. Saute onion for two minutes. Add chicken stock and bring to a boil.

Turn heat down to simmer. Add corn, cobs, cumin, coriander, and salt. Simmer for 15 minutes. Remove from heat. Remove 2 t corn kernels from pot, set aside.

Remove cobs, pour remaining soup into a blender. Pulse until smooth.

Stir in half-and-half, reserved corn kernels, and chives. Salt and pepper to taste.

JEWISH PENICILLIN PLUS

2 T magic butter
4 carrots, peeled and chopped
2 celery stalks, chopped
1 small onion, diced
2 cloves garlic, crushed
1 t tumeric
2 T flour
3-4 c chicken, cooked, shredded
4 qts chicken stock
3 c egg noodles
1 sprig rosemary
2 sprigs parsley
Ample salt and pepper to taste

Melt butter in large Dutch oven over medium heat. Add vegetables, cook until softened and onion is translucent, 5-7 minutes.

Add tumeric and flour to coat vegetable mix. Add chicken, stock, and seasonings.

Simmer until soup flavors are combined, 30-45 minutes. Stir in egg noodles and cook until tender, ~10 minutes more.

LASAGNA SOUP

1 T magic oil
1½ # sausage
½ onion, diced
1 small zucchini, diced
2 cloves garlic, minced
1 t oregano
½ t red pepper flakes
2 T tomato paste
1 lg can crushed tomatoes
4 c chicken broth
2 c spinach leaves
6 oz lasagna noodles, cooked per directions, cut into bite-size pieces
Parmesan or ricotta cheese for garnish

Heat oil over medium heat. Add sausage, break up while cooking. Cook until brown.

Add onions and zucchini, cook another 5 minutes.

Add garlic, oregano, and red pepper flakes. Stir.

Add tomato paste and cook for another 4-5 minutes. Add crushed tomatoes and chicken broth, simmer for 20 minutes.

Add fresh spinach leaves and cooked lasagna noodle pieces. Stir until spinach leaves wilt.

Garnish with grated parmesan and a dollop of ricotta.

RICE AND TURKEY

2 T magic oil
¾ c brown rice
2 carrots, chopped
2 cloves garlic, minced
1 # ground turkey
4 c chicken broth
2 c chopped kale
1 t garlic powder
1 t onion powder
3 T fresh parsley, finely chopped

In a saucepan, bring rice and 1½ c water to a boil over high heat. Cover, reduce heat to low. Simmer until rice is tender, ~30 minutes.

Warm oil in a large pan over medium heat. Sauté carrots, stirring occasionally, until tender. Add garlic, sauté together for 30 seconds.

Transfer carrot mixture to a bowl. Add turkey to saucepan, season with salt and pepper.   Cook, stirring to break up sausage, until no longer pink, ~5 minutes.

Add broth, rice, carrot mixture, kale, garlic powder, and onion powder to the pan. Stir and bring to a boil over high heat.

Reduce heat to medium and simmer until rice is tender, ~5 minutes.

Garnish with parsley.

VEGGIE BOWL

2 T magic oil
1 c cauliflower, chunked
1 bell pepper, diced
1 small onion, chopped
3 carrots, sliced
2 stalks celery, chopped
2 c diced tomatoes
2 bay leaves
¼ c chopped parsley
7 c vegetable stock

Heat oil on medium. Add vegetables, parsley, bay leaves, and vegetable stock.

Bring the soup to a boil, then simmer 20 minutes.

Season with salt and pepper to taste.

WILD 'SHROOM SOUP

2 T magic butter
3 cloves garlic, finely chopped
2 c fresh mushrooms
1 T fresh thyme
1 bay leaf
1 t Worcestershire sauce
1 c chicken or vegetable stock
1 T flour dissolved in 1 T water
½ c heavy cream
½ c milk
Dash of nutmeg

Melt butter and lightly sauté garlic on medium heat.

Add mushrooms, thyme, bay leaf, and Worcestershire sauce. Cook until moisture from mushrooms evaporates, ~5 minutes.

Add chicken broth. Stir occasionally until broth boils, then reduce and simmer for ten minutes.

Add diluted flour, stirring constantly, until soup thickens. Season with salt and nutmeg. Add cream and milk, simmer for five minutes.

Serve with fresh ground pepper, garnish with fresh parsley or chives.

SWEETS

Apple Weed Wedges

Chocolate Kief Cookies

Florentines

Fruity Triangles

In Your Buckeyes

Peachy Melba Shortcake

Puff Puff Pass Petit Fours

Spiced Shortbread Nugs

Trippin' Trifle

APPLE WEED WEDGES

1 c magic butter
2¼ brown sugar
Pinch of salt
1 c light corn syrup
1 can sweetened condensed milk
1 t vanilla
6 apples

Melt butter in a saucepan, add brown sugar and salt. Stir until combined.

Stir in corn syrup.

Gradually add sweetened condensed milk, stirring continuously.

Cook and stir over medium heat until candy reaches firm ball stage (245 degrees), about 12-15 minutes.

Remove from heat. Stir in vanilla.

Cut apples in half and hollow out, leaving ½" flesh under the skin. Set halves in a muffin tin for balance.

Fill apple halves with caramel mixture. Allow to cool.

Once caramel is set in apple halves, slice into wedges.

CHOCOLATE KIEF COOKIES

2 c magic butter
2 c flour
1 t baking soda
½ t baking powder
1 t salt
½ c sugar
½ c brown sugar
1 t vanilla extract
2 eggs
2 c chocolate chips
1 c finely chopped nuts (optional)

Preheat oven to 375.

In one bowl, mix flour, baking soda, baking powder, and salt.

In another larger bowl, mix magic butter with sugars until creamy. Add vanilla and eggs, one at a time, beating all the while.

Slowly add flour mixture to larger bowl, mixing thoroughly.

Add chocolate chips and nuts.

Divide dough mixture into six balls and place them on a lightly greased cookie sheet.

Bake 10-12 minutes or until golden brown. Remove from oven and cool on a wire rack.

FLORENTINES

½ c magic butter, plus 2 T magic butter
½ c milk
¼ c sugar
1 c chopped almonds, toasted
¾ c diced mixed candied fruits and peels
1 t finely shredded orange peel
¼ c flour
¾ c semisweet chocolate pieces

Preheat oven to 350.

In a medium heavy saucepan, combine ½ c butter, milk, and sugar. Bring to a full rolling boil, stirring occasionally. Remove from heat.

Stir in almonds, candied fruits and peels, and orange peel.

Stir in flour.

Drop batter from a level tablespoon onto a greased and floured cookie sheet (re-grease and flour between batches). Flatten batter into 3" circles.

Bake for 8-10 minutes or until edges are lightly browned. Cool on cookie sheet for one minute, then remove cookies and cool on waxed paper.

In a small heavy saucepan, heat chocolate pieces and 2 T butter over low heat until just melted, stirring occasionally. Spread a scant teaspoon of chocolate mixture evenly over the bottom of each cookie. When chocolate is almost set, use the tines of a fork to draw wavy lines through the chocolate.

FRUITY TRIANGLES

¼ c magic butter
½ c sugar
½ c evaporated milk
1 c coarsely chopped candied cherries
¼ c coarsely chopped candied pineapple
¾ c sliced almonds
2 t finely shredded orange peel
1 tube refrigerated sugar cookie dough
Powdered sugar

Preheat oven to 375.

Flatten cookie dough into lightly greased baking pan. Bake until light brown, ~15 minutes.

In a medium saucepan, combine sugar, evaporated milk, and butter. Bring to a boil for one minute, stirring constantly.

Remove from heat. Add cherries, pineapple, almonds, and orange peel. Gently stir until completely coated.

Spread fruit mixture on top of baked cookie crust. Bake for 15-18 minutes or until top is golden.

Cool in pan on a wire rack.

Sift powdered sugar over top. Cut into triangle-shaped bars.

IN YOUR BUCKEYES

¼ c magic butter, plus 1 t, divided
1 jar peanut butter
1 box powdered sugar
1 pkg chocolate chips

Combine ¼ c softened butter with peanut butter and powdered sugar.

Allow to chill in refrigerator.

Line a baking sheet with waxed paper. Roll into 1" balls and return to refrigerator.

Melt chocolate and 1 t butter together in a double boiler over medium heat. Whisk until smooth.

Dip a toothpick into each ball and dip in chocolate mixture.

Place on waxed paper and allow to set in refrigerator.

PEACHY MELBA SHORTCAKES

6 T magic butter, divided
3 T sugar
½ c milk
2¼ c baking mix
½ c raspberry preserves
1 can sliced peaches in heavy syrup
1 container frozen whipped cream

Preheat oven to 425.

Cream 3 T magic butter with sugar. Add milk and baking mix. Combine until a pliable mix develops.

Form into six biscuits and bake on an ungreased baking sheet for 10-12 minutes or until tops are golden brown.

In a saucepan, melt remaining 3 T magic butter over medium-low heat. Add preserves and whisk vigorously.

Simmer on low for five minutes, being careful not to burn. Remove from heat to cool.

Slice biscuits in half, spreading liberally with whipped cream.

Layer peaches on top of whipped cream. Drizzle with raspberry sauce.

Top with other half of biscuit and a dollop of whipped cream.

Garnish with fresh raspberries and a mint sprig.

PUFF PUFF PASS PETIT FOURS

2 c magic butter
1 # almond paste
1 c sugar
1 t almond extract
6 eggs
1 c flour
Pinch salt
Raspberry preserves
6 T corn syrup
2 T almond extract
17½ c powdered sugar (yes, 17½; ~5 boxes)
Green food coloring

Preheat oven to 375.

Mix almond paste and sugar until well combined.   Add almond extract, mix. Slowly add butter, beat until light and fluffy. Add eggs, one at a time, beating to combine after each.   Add flour and salt and beat until combined.

Divide the batter between two prepared baking sheets, ~2¼ cups each sheet.

Spread with a spatula, checking for air pockets. Bake 15-20 minutes, testing with a toothpick. Cool on wire racks.

Spread raspberry preserves between cake layers. Using two baking sheets, weigh down with large cans. Refrigerate for at least an hour.

For icing: Combine 1¼ cups water with corn syrup and almond extract. Slowly whisk in powdered sugar. Tint as desired. Put bowl in a pan semi-filled with water to double boil.

Cut cake into 1" squares. Place on wire rack ½" apart. Pour tinted frosting over cake pieces. Let stand until set, about 30 minutes.

SPICED SHORTBREAD NUGS

½ c magic butter
1 ¼ c flour
¼ c brown sugar
½ t aniseed, crushed
¼ t ground cinnamon
¼ t ground cloves
¼ t ground cardamom

In a mixing bowl, stir together flour, sugar, and spices. Cut in butter until mixture resembles fine crumbs. Form mixture into a ball and knead until smooth.

Divide dough into 12 portions. On a lightly floured surface, roll each portion of dough into a 10" long rope. Cut ropes into ½" long pieces.

Place pieces ½" apart on ungreased baking pan. Bake 12-15 minutes or until edges are firm and bottoms are lightly browned.

Remove cookies, cool on paper towels.

TRIPPIN' TRIFLE

1 t magic butter
Magic oil (as much as is needed in the...)
1 box of brownie mix
1 can sweetened condensed milk
2 c whole milk
1 box chocolate pudding mix
1 pt frozen whipped topping
1 pkg chocolate graham crackers

Fill a saucepan with water. Place the unopened can of sweetened condensed milk in the saucepan and simmer on low for an hour.

Bake brownie mix according to instructions on the box, substituting the magic oil.

Simmer milk for thirty minutes with magic butter. Be careful not to scald.

Set aside to cool.

Mix pudding following directions on the box, substituting magic milk.

In a trifle bowl, layer crumbled brownies then a drizzle of the caramelized dulce de leche made from the sweetened condensed milk.

For the next layer, crumble chocolate graham crackers in your hands. Sprinkle in a layer about ½" thick.

Spread a layer of the pudding, top that with a layer of whipped topping.

Repeat the layering process: brownies, drizzle, crumble, pudding, whipped. Then crumble a few more crackers really small to garnish the top of the trifle.

Grab a spoon.

INDEX

Apple Weed Wedges 97

Baked Bacon Dip 21
Baked Banana Smoothie 11
Beyond Baked Beans 59
Biscuit Pot Pie 31
Bloody MaryJane 12
Broccoli Bud Casserole 60
Broc-Pot-Leek Soup 81
Budder Beer 13
Buttered Bhang 14

Cabbage Comfort 83
Caramel Assault 49
Caramel Corn Crack 69
Cheesy French Onion 84
Chicken Enchiladas with Green Sauce 33
Chocolate Kief Cookies 99
Corn Cob Chowder 86
Cranked-Up Carbonara 35
Creamy Guac 22

Doobie Dogs 37

Easy Cheesy Ball 23

Florentines   101
Fluffer Snicker Firecrackers   71
Fried Potatoes   61
Fruity Triangles   103

Garlic Cheese Bread   72

High Chai   15
Hummus Ho   24

In Your Buckeyes   105

Jerk Pork   38
Jewish Penicillin Plus   87

Kickin' Hot Sauce   51

Lasagna Soup   88
Loco Coconut Milk   16

Magic Manicotti   40
Monster Milkshake   17

Nutty Oat Bars   73

Oh Corn   62

Peach Barbeque Sauce   53
Peachy Melba Shortcake   106

Peanut Sauce   54
Pepperoni Rolls   74
Pizza Dip in 30 Minutes or Less   25
Poppin' Jalapeno Popper Dip   26
Porky Pig Medallions   42
Pot Hot Chocolate   18
Puff Puff Pass Petit Fours   108

Quinoa Wow   64

Rice and Turkey   90
Righteous Red Sauce   55
Roasted Green Beans   65

Smoked Pimento Cheese   27
Something Fishy   28
Snoop Diddy   19
Spiced Shortbread Nugs   110
Spicy Peanuts   75
Spreadin' Crab   29
Sticky Wings   43
Stir Fried Sauce   56
Super Fried Rice   45
Sweet Sweet Potato Sticks   66

Totally Grilled Squash   67
Trippin' Trifle   111

Unbelievable Pesto   57

Veggie Bowl   92

Wild 'Shroom Soup   93
Wonton Crackers   76

You Say Potato 1   77
You Say Potato 2   78

45302390R00068

Made in the USA
Charleston, SC
15 August 2015